Marjoleine's
Embroidered Cards

G000241582

Marjolein Zweed
Caroline van Ravesteijn

FORTE PUBLISHERS

Contents

© 2004 Forte Uitgevers, Utrecht
© 2004 for the translation by the publisher
Original title:
Marjoleine's borduurkaarten

All rights reserved.
No part of this publication may be copied, stored in an electronic file or made public, in any form or in any way whatsoever, either electronically, mechanically, by photocopying or any other form of recording, without the publisher's prior written permission.

ISBN 90 5877 456 2

This is a publication from
Forte Publishers BV
P.O. Box 1394
3500 BJ Utrecht
The Netherlands

For more information about the creative books available from
Forte Uitgevers:
www.forteuitgevers.nl

Final editing: Gina Kors-Lambers, Steenwijk, the Netherlands
Photography and digital image editing: Fotografie Gerhard Witteveen, Apeldoorn, the Netherlands
Cover and inner design:
BADE creatieve communicatie, Baarn, the Netherlands
Translation: Michael Ford, TextCase, Hilversum, the Netherlands

Preface

A number of books have already been published on how to make cards using Marjoleine's drawings. The publisher had the idea to make embroidery patterns from Marjoleine's drawings. Caroline started transforming the drawings into embroidery patterns with great enthusiasm. Marjolein then used the embroidery to make cards. This cooperation resulted in a number of beautiful cards which you can find in this book.

Have fun with the embroidery and the cards.

Good luck.

Marjolein   *Caroline*

Techniques

Embroidery

All the embroidery is in cross stitch on cloth with 6.4 bundles of thread per centimetre (Coats: Aida 355 cream). Take into account that the result may be larger or smaller when using different embroidery cloth. Use a piece of embroidery cloth which is larger than the desired result, because that is nicer to work with, and cut it to the right size when you have finished.
Use 30 to 50 cm of thread. The embroidery silk consists of six threads. Split off two threads to start embroidering. Place the remaining four threads on a piece of card with holes and write down the colour number and the pattern symbol, so that you can easily find it again when you continue at a later time. See the first step-by-step photograph.

The colour lists for the patterns use the DMC numbers. A conversion lists from DMC numbers to Anchor numbers is given in the *Materials* chapter.

Use two threads of embroidery silk and start in the middle of the pattern. Use an embroidery needle with a blunt point (no. 24 or 26) for the cross stitches. Insert this in the existing holes around the bundles of thread of the Aida cloth.

Attach the thread by looping the first stitch over the thread, as shown on the far left of the first step-by-step photograph. Note: do this on the back of the embroidery! Next to that on the photograph, you can see how to make lines from the bottom to the top. You then go from the top to the bottom to complete the cross-stitch. You can see this on the next line on the photograph. You can also embroider from left to right, but make sure all the top threads face the same direction. This applies to all the colours and, therefore, the entire embroidery.

Use a needle with a sharp point for the back-stitch. You can insert it where you wish and, therefore, follow the pattern correctly. You can see this on the far right of the first step-by-step photograph. The backstitches are made with 1/6 thread, unless otherwise stated, such as for the nose of the bear which is embroidered with 2/6 thread. All the backstitches are indicated by a continuous line on the pattern. Pay good attention! The colours used vary and are stated with every colour list. For example, see the church on the second step-by-step photograph. The backstitch of the church is made with colour no. 318, whilst the clock and the windows are made with colour no. 3799.

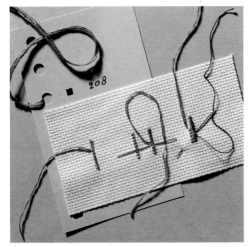

1. Attaching, cross-stitching and backstitching.

2. The backstitches are made with different colours.

3. Stick double-sided adhesive tape around the opening in the card.

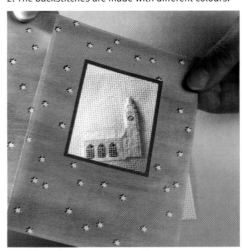

4. Stick the embroidery behind the opening.

Gold thread is used for the Christmas decorations and silver thread is used to produce a sparkling effect. Use a short thread for this, because the thread splits easily.

Once the embroidery is finished, press it with a damp cloth.

Card and pattern paper

Openings are cut in the pattern paper and the card. Since the dimensions differ slightly, subtle, narrow borders are produced. Carefully select the card colour. The right colour combinations of card, pattern paper and embroidery are what make the cards attractive. It is best to cut the card and the pattern paper using a knife and a ruler.

Once you have cut an opening in the card, stick double-sided adhesive tape around the opening at the back as shown in the third step-by-step photograph. Next, stick the embroidery on the card with the aid of the double-sided adhesive tape. This is easiest if you look through the opening as shown in the fourth step-by-step photograph, because you can then see whether it will be stuck in the right place. It is best to use photo glue when sticking the other materials

together, because if you spill this glue, it can be easily wiped away. Use 3D glue or foam tape if you wish to give more depth to what you stick on the card. Try and find out what you prefer, because this is often a personal choice.

If you use 3D glue, it is best to put it in a syringe so that it is easier to apply. Apply small drops of 3D glue to the back of the picture and carefully stick the picture on the card. Do not press too hard, otherwise you will loose the depth. You must allow the glue to dry properly before posting the card. Foam tape can be bought in squares or on a roll, so that you can cut it yourself into small pieces and then stick them on the back of the picture. Make sure you stick the picture in the right place, because you will not be able to move it about once you have stuck it down.

The patterns must be increased in size by 143%.

Materials

- ❏ Cloth:
  Aida 6.4 bundles of
  thread per centimetre
  (Coats: Aida C.355
  cream)
- ❏ Needles: embroidery
  needle no. 24 or 26
  (blunt point) and a
  sewing needle with
  a sharp point
- ❏ Embroidery silk: DMC
- ❏ 3D scissors

- ❏ Knife and cutting mat
- ❏ Transparent cutting
  ruler (Securit)
- ❏ Photo glue
- ❏ 3D glue and a syringe
- ❏ 3D foam tape
- ❏ Marjoleine's
  3D cutting sheets
- ❏ Marjoleine's
  pattern paper
- ❏ Marjoleine's
  scrapbook paper

- ❏ Papicolor card
  You can use this card to make your own cards.
  You can also buy pre-cut and pre-folded standard
  and square cards. The colour numbers are stated
  in each chapter.
- ❏ Double-sided adhesive tape
  Use double-sided adhesive tape to stick the
  embroidery in the opening. Double-sided adhesive
  tape is available in different colours.
- ❏ Eyelet tools, mini eyelet toolkit, eyelet mat and
  a hammer

The other materials are listed in the chapters in
which they are used.

List of all the DMC and/or Anchor colours used

DMC	Anchor	DMC	Anchor
B5200	1	826	146
White	2	827	128
153	95	830	889
208	98	831	888
209	97	833	887
210	96	839	1086
211	95	841	1082
223	895	931	977
224	894	932	976
310	403	937	268
318	235	976	803
322	146	3046	887
334	136	3051	268
414	235	3053	260
415	234	3072	847
420	375	3078	292
434	370	3743	869
436	369	3747	117
437	368	3753	128
543	933	3755	144
611	898	3756	1037
612	831	3799	401
666	46	3823	386
676	942	3841	128
677	886	3862	1086
738	367	3863	1084
739	276	3042	870
746	275		
762	397		
778	1016	Gold and Silver thread	
782	309		
801	358		
813	129		

Violets

The violets in my garden

always seem to look at me

as I walk past.

What you need:
• Pattern paper no. 9 • Scrapbook paper: princess/angel and golden brown patchwork • Papicolor card: purple (46) • Waxed cord: natural (2 mm) • Parchment paper • White text sticker • Eyelets: mini ivory

Card 1

Take a piece of pattern paper (21 x 15 cm) and fold it double. Draw a square (5.5 x 5.5 cm) on the back 1.5 cm from the side and 1.5 cm from the top and cut it out. Stick purple card (14.5 x 10 cm) against the pattern paper. Cut a square out of the purple card so that a small, purple border protrudes from the pattern paper. Stick the embroidery behind the opening. Stick the pattern paper on a purple double card (10.5 x 15 cm). Make a pink label, stick it on purple card and cut it out leaving a small border. Stick a sticker on the label and use 3D glue or foam tape to add some buttons. Take 25 cm of cord, thread it through the label and tie a knot in it.

Use foam tape or 3D glue to stick the label on the card.

Card 2

Take a piece of pattern paper (21 x 15 cm) and fold it double. Draw a square (6 x 6 cm) on the back 1.5 cm from the side and 4 cm from the top and cut it out. Stick purple card (14.5 x 10 cm) against the pattern paper. Cut a square out of the purple card so that a small, purple border protrudes from the pattern paper. Stick the embroidery behind the opening. Stick the pattern paper on a purple double card (10.5 x 15 cm). Stick two large pieces of patchwork paper on the card and use 3D glue or foam tape to stick a button on the top piece of patchwork paper. Stick a text sticker on parchment paper and tear it out leaving a border (this is best done by placing a ruler on the parchment paper and tearing along the ruler). Use eyelets to attach this strip to the card.

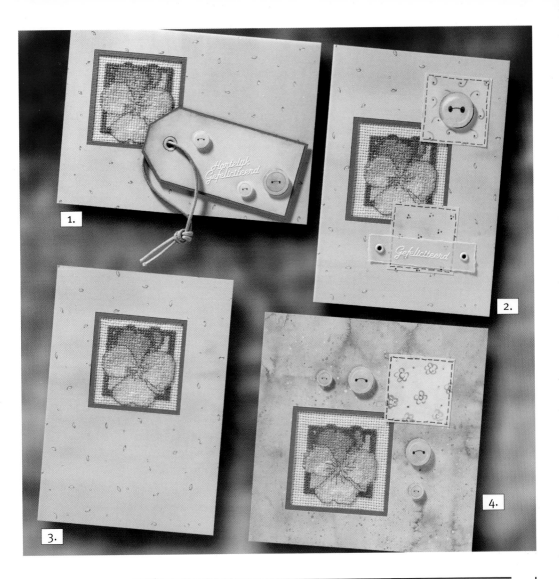

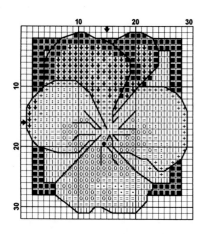

Violet colour list

·	white	●	976
■	208	O	3078
↓	209	:	3743
+	210	=	3823
I	211		

Backstitch 1/6 thread: 208

Card 3

Take a piece of pattern paper (21 x 15 cm) and fold it double. Draw a square (5.5 x 5.5 cm) on the back 2.5 cm from the sides and 2.5 cm from the top and cut it out. Stick purple card (14.5 x 10 cm) against the pattern paper. Cut a square out of the purple card so that a small, purple border protrudes from the pattern paper. Stick the embroidery behind the opening. Stick the pattern paper on a purple double card (10.5 x 15 cm).

Card 4

Take a piece of pattern paper (13 x 13 cm). Draw a square (6 x 6 cm) on the back 2 cm from the side and 2 cm from the bottom and cut it out. Stick purple card (12.5 x 12.5 cm) against the pattern paper. Cut a square out of the purple card so that a small, purple border protrudes from the pattern paper. Stick the embroidery behind the opening. Stick the pattern paper on a square double card (13 x 13 cm). Stick a piece of patchwork paper on the card. Use 3D glue or foam tape to stick some buttons on the card.

Watering can with butterflies

Sun, summer, the multitude
of colours and butterflies that
brighten up the day.

What you need:
- *Pattern paper no. 10 • 3D cutting sheet:*
daisies • Scrapbook paper: blue patchwork
- *Papicolor card: night blue (41) and lavender (21)*

Card 1

Take a piece of pattern paper (21 x 15 cm) and
fold it double. Draw two rectangles (6.5 x
5.5 cm and 4.5 x 2.5 cm) on the back 1.5 cm
from the side and cut them out. Stick night blue
card (14.5 x 10 cm) against the pattern paper.
Cut two rectangles out of the night blue card
so that small, night blue borders protrude from
the pattern paper. Stick the embroideries
behind the openings. Stick the pattern paper
on a lavender double card (10.5 x 15 cm).

Card 2

Cut a square (13 x 13 cm) out of the pattern
paper and a square (12.5 x 12.5 cm) out of night
blue card. Draw a line around the back of both
squares 3 cm from the sides and cut out the

squares. Since the night blue square is slightly
smaller, the opening will also be slightly
smaller, which gives a subtle border. Stick the

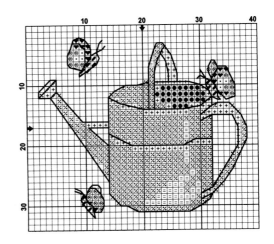

Watering can and butterflies colour list

•	white	♥	813
=	3756	❚	831
✕	3753		
+	932		*Backstitch 1/6 thread*
●	931		*Watering can: 931*
◉	827		*Wings: 813*
			Bodies: 830

two frames on top of each other. Stick the embroidery behind the opening. Stick everything on a lavender double card (13 x 13 cm). Use 3D glue or foam tape to stick a butterfly and a daisy on the card.

Card 3

Cut a square (13 x 13 cm) out of the pattern paper and stick it on a square lavender double card (13 x 13 cm). Cut another square (10.5 x 10.5 cm) out of the pattern paper. Draw two squares (4 x 4 cm) on the back of this 1 cm from the sides and cut them out. Cut a square (11 x 11 cm) out of night blue card and stick the pattern paper with the two openings in it on top. Cut two squares out of the night blue card so that small, night blue borders protrude from the pattern paper. Stick the embroideries behind the openings. Stick everything on the card. Stick two pictures of daisies (middle size) on the card. Use 3D glue or foam tape to stick two daisies on the pictures to make the daisies 3D.

Card 4

Fold a piece of pattern paper (15 x 21 cm) double. Stick a piece of night blue card (12.5 x 8.5 cm) and a piece of pattern paper (12 x 8 cm) on the pattern paper. Stick pieces of patchwork paper and a picture of a daisy (middle size) on top. Cut out some squares (2 x 2 cm) and stick the embroideries behind them. Stick the pattern paper on a lavender double card (10.5 x 15 cm). Use 3D glue or foam tape to stick some buttons and a cut out daisy on the card.

1.

2.

3.

4.

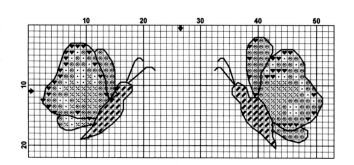

Butterfly colour list

•	White
✕	3753
⊙	827
♥	813
◣	831

Backstitch 1/6 thread
Wings: 813
Bodies: 830

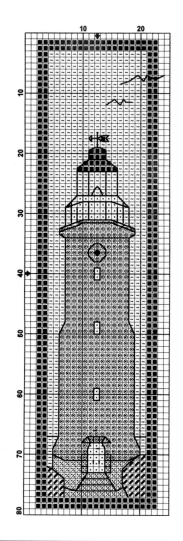

Lighthouse colour list

•	white	⊙	437
●	310	■	666
—	415	~	762
✕	436	◣	937

Backstitch 1/6 thread
Birds, door, dome and wind vane: 3799
Lighthouse: 434
Fence: 318

The beach

Sun, sea and sand with the wind blowing through your hair; that's a feeling you would like to hold on to for ever.

What you need:
- *Pattern paper no. 16 • 3D cutting sheet: beach*
- *Scrapbook paper: blue patchwork • Papicolor card: night blue (41) and fiesta red (12) • Mini eyelets: red • White border sticker*

Card 1

Take a night blue double card (10.5 x 15 cm). Cut a strip from the front of the card to that the front is 6 cm wide. Stick a piece of pattern paper (15 x 16.5 cm) around the card. Draw a line around the back of the front flap of the card 1.5 cm from the edge and cut out the rectangle. Cut a rectangle (6 x 15 cm) out of the fiesta red card and stick the card against the back of the front flap of the card. Cut out a rectangle to leave a narrow, red border. Stick the embroidery behind the opening. Stick part of a tassel on the card and fold the excess behind the card. Use 3D glue or foam tape to stick a button on the card.

Card 2

Cut a piece of pattern paper (12 x 8 cm). Draw a rectangle (6 x 4 cm) on the back 2 cm from the top, bottom and side and cut it out. Stick fiesta red card (12.5 x 8.5 cm) against the pattern paper. Cut a rectangle out of the fiesta red card so that a small, fiesta red border protrudes from the pattern paper. Stick the embroidery behind the opening. Take a night blue double card (10.5 x 15 cm). Fold a strip of pattern sheet (15 x 21 cm) double and stick it

around the card. Stick the frame on the card. Stick pieces of patchwork paper on the card. Use 3D glue or foam tape to stick buttons on the card.

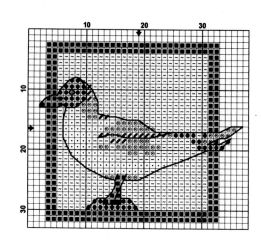

Gull colour list

•	white	●	839
—	415	o	310 (eye)
⊙	318	■	666
◢	414	~	762

Backstitch 1/6 thread: 3799
Stitch four white backstitches around the
eye to make a white circle.

Card 3

Take a night blue double card (13 x 13 cm).
Fold a strip of pattern paper (26 x 13 cm) double
and stick it around the card. Stick a white frame
(sticker) on the card 3 cm from the side. Draw a
square (5.5 x 5.5 cm) on the back of the card
2.5 cm from the side and the bottom and cut it
out. Stick the embroidery behind the opening.
Stick a picture of a sailing boat (middle size)
on the card. Use 3D glue or foam tape to stick
some buttons and a cut out sailing boat
on the card.

Card 4

Cut a rectangle (14.8 x 6 cm) out of pattern
paper. Draw a rectangle on the back 1.5 cm from
the sides and cut it out. Cut a rectangle (15.3 x
6.5 cm) out of fiesta red card and stick the
frame on top. Cut out the inside of the frame to
leave a narrow, red border. Stick the embroidery
behind the opening. Punch eyelets in the cor-
ners. Cut a square (21 x 21 cm) from night blue
card and fold it double. Fold a strip of pattern
paper (21 x 21 cm) double and stick it around
the card. Stick the frame on top.

1.

2.

3.

4.

Teddy bears

Every birth deserves
congratulating, so send
the happy parents an
attractive card.

What you need:
• Pattern paper: no. 7 and no. 8 • Scrapbook
paper: patchwork alphabet, blue bears and pink
bears • Papicolor card: pale pink (23), cerise
(33), lavender (21) and night blue (41)

Card 1

Take a piece of pattern paper no. 8 (21 x 15 cm)
and fold it double. Draw a rectangle on the
back 4 cm from the bottom and 2 cm from the
other sides and cut it out. Stick cerise card
(14.5 x 10 cm) against the pattern paper. Cut a
rectangle out of the cerise card so that a small,
cerise border protrudes from the pattern paper.
Stick the embroidery behind the opening.
Stick the pattern paper on a pale pink double
card (10.5 x 15 cm). Cut out the letters of the
name. Stick them on cerise card and cut them
out leaving a small border. Use 3D glue or
foam tape to stick the letters and a bow on the
card.

Card 2

Take a piece of pattern paper no. 8 (13 x 13).
Draw a square on the back 2 cm from all the
sides and cut it out. Stick cerise card (12.5 x
12.5 cm) against the pattern paper. Cut a square
out of the cerise card so that a small, cerise
border protrudes from the pattern paper. Stick
the embroidery behind the opening. Stick the
pattern paper on a square, pale pink double
card (13 x 13 cm). Stick a piece of patchwork
paper on the card and use 3D glue or foam tape
to stick a button on it.

Card 3

Take a piece of pattern paper no. 7 (13 x 13).
Draw a square on the back 2 cm from all the
sides and cut it out. Stick night blue card (12.5 x
12.5 cm) against the pattern paper. Cut a square
out of the night blue card so that a small, night
blue border protrudes from the pattern paper.
Stick the embroidery behind the opening. Stick
the pattern paper on a square, lavender double
card (13 x 13 cm). Cut out the letters of the
name. Stick them on night blue card and cut
them out leaving a small border. Use 3D glue
or foam tape to stick the letters on the card.

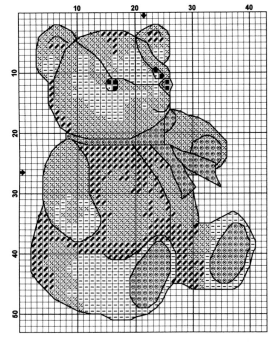

Blue bear colour list

▪	white	⁒	3863
⊙	932	❰	3862
—	841	■	310

Backstitch 1/6 thread
Bear: 839
Around the blue: 931
2/6 thread around the eyes and nose: 310

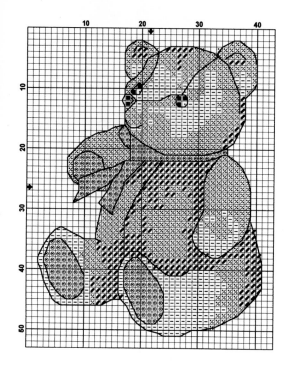

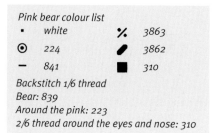

Pink bear colour list
- white   % 3863
- ⊙ 224   ❢ 3862
- — 841   ■ 310

Backstitch 1/6 thread
Bear: 839
Around the pink: 223
2/6 thread around the eyes and nose: 310

Card 4

Take a piece of pattern paper no. 7 (21 x 15 cm) and fold it double. Draw a rectangle on the back 4 cm from the bottom and 2 cm from the other sides and cut it out. Stick night blue card (14.5 x 10 cm) against the pattern paper. Cut a rectangle out of the night blue card so that a small, night blue border protrudes from the pattern paper. Stick the embroidery behind the opening. Stick the pattern paper on a lavender double card (10.5 x 15 cm). Use 3D glue or foam tape to stick buttons on the card.

1.

2.

3.

4.

Tea

Spoil somebody by offering

them a cup of tea.

What you need:
• Scrapbook paper: brown alphabet, golden brown patchwork and blue patchwork
• Pattern paper no. 12 • Papicolor card: nut brown (39) and carnation white (03) •
Waxed cord: natural (2 mm) • Gold text sticker: Many congratulations • Mini eyelets: ivory

Card 1

Take a piece of pattern paper (13 x 13 cm). Draw a square (6 x 6 cm) on the back 1.5 cm from the side and 1.5 cm from the bottom. Draw another square (4 x 4 cm) on the back in a different corner 1.5 cm from the side and 1.5 cm from the top. Cut out the squares. Stick nut brown card (12.5 x 12.5 cm) against the pattern paper. Cut two squares out of the nut brown card so that small, nut brown borders protrude from the pattern paper. Stick the embroideries behind the openings. Stick the pattern paper on a square, carnation white double card (13 x 13 cm). Use 3D glue or foam tape to stick four buttons on the card.

Card 2

Take a piece of pattern paper (21 x 15 cm) and fold it double. Draw a rectangle on the back 4 cm from the bottom and 2 cm from the other sides and cut it out. Stick nut brown card (14.5 x 10 cm) against the pattern paper. Cut a rectangle out of the nut brown card so that a small, nut brown border protrudes from the pattern paper. Stick the embroidery behind the opening. Take a strip of nut brown card (10.7 x 2.4 cm) and stick the letters T, E and A on it. Stick this strip on the pattern paper under the embroidery. Punch two eyelets at both ends of the strip. Stick the pattern paper on a carnation white double card (10.5 x 15 cm).

Card 3

Take a piece of pattern paper (21 x 15 cm) and fold it double. Draw a square (4.5 x 4.5 cm) on the back 2 cm from the side and 2 cm from the top and cut it out. Stick nut brown card (14.5 x 10 cm) against the pattern paper. Cut a square out of the nut brown card so that a small, nut brown border protrudes from the pattern paper. Stick the embroidery behind the opening. Stick the pattern paper on a carnation white double card (10.5 x 15 cm). Make a blue label, stick it on nut brown card and cut it out leaving a small

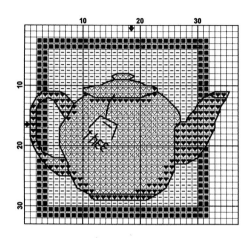

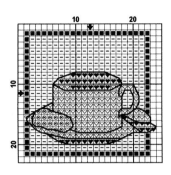

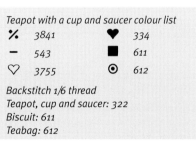

Teapot with a cup and saucer colour list

%	3841	**♥**	334
−	543	**■**	611
♡	3755	**⊙**	612

Backstitch 1/6 thread
Teapot, cup and saucer: 322
Biscuit: 611
Teabag: 612

border. Stick a text sticker on the label and use some 3D glue or foam tape to add some buttons. Cut 25 cm of cord, thread it through the label and tie a knot in it. Use foam tape or 3D glue to stick the label on the card.

Card 4

Cut a square (13 x 13 cm) out of pattern paper and stick it on a square, carnation white double card (13 x 13 cm). Cut another square (10 x 10 cm) out of the pattern paper. Draw a square (6 x 6 cm) on the back of this 2 cm from the sides and cut it out. Cut a square (10.5 x 10.5 cm) out of nut brown card and stick it

against the pattern paper. Cut a square out of the nut brown card so that a small, nut brown border protrudes from the pattern paper. Stick the embroidery behind the opening. Stick everything on the card. Use 3D glue or foam tape to stick four buttons on the card.

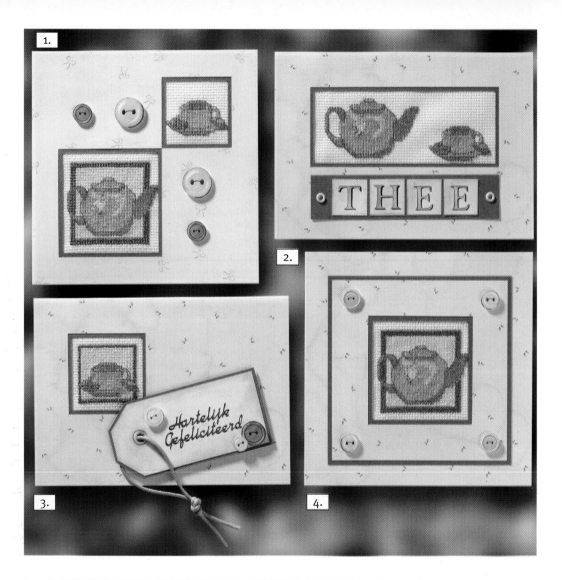

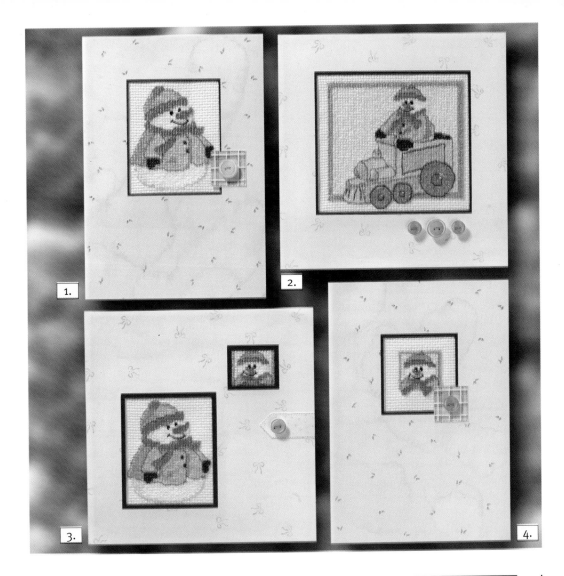

Snowmen

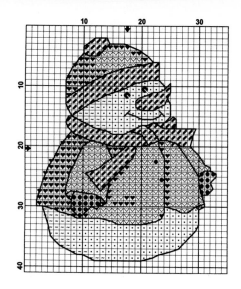

Embroider these snowmen in
their train for all children
young and old.

What you need:
• *3D cutting sheet: snowmen • Pattern paper
no. 12 • Papicolor card: night blue (41) and
carnation white (03)*

Card 1

Take a piece of pattern paper (21 x 15 cm) and
fold it double. Draw a rectangle (5.5 x 6.5 cm)
on the back 2.5 cm from the sides and the top
and cut it out. Stick night blue card (14.5 x
10 cm) against the pattern paper. Cut a square
out of the night blue card so that a small, night
blue border protrudes from the pattern paper.
Stick the embroidery behind the opening. Stick
the pattern paper on a carnation white double
card (10.5 x 15 cm). Stick a piece of patchwork
paper on the card. Use 3D glue or foam tape to
stick a button on the piece of patchwork paper.

Card 2

Take a piece of pattern paper (13 x 13 cm).
Draw a rectangle (9 x 8 cm) on the back

2 cm from the sides and 2 cm from the top
and cut it out. Stick night blue card (12.5 x
12.5 cm) against the pattern paper. Cut a
rectangle out of the night blue card so that a
small, night blue border protrudes from the
pattern paper. Stick the embroidery behind the
opening. Stick the pattern paper on a square,
carnation white double card (13 x 13 cm). Use
3D glue or foam tape to stick three buttons on
the card.

Card 3

Take a piece of pattern paper (13 x 13 cm).
Draw a rectangle (5.5 x 6.5 cm) on the back
2 cm from the side and 2 cm from the bottom.
Draw another rectangle (3 x 2.5 cm) on the

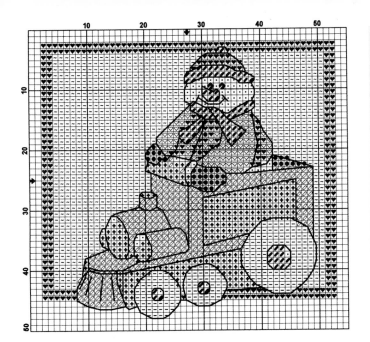

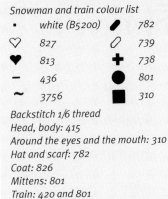

Snowman and train colour list

•	white (B5200)	✦	782
♡	827	⃠	739
♥	813	✛	738
—	436	●	801
~	3756	■	310

Backstitch 1/6 thread
Head, body: 415
Around the eyes and the mouth: 310
Hat and scarf: 782
Coat: 826
Mittens: 801
Train: 420 and 801

Finally, add a small amount of white
to the eyes.

back in a different corner 2 cm from the side
and 2 cm from the top. Cut out the rectangles.
Stick night blue card (12.5 x 12.5 cm) against
the pattern paper. Cut two rectangles out of the
night blue card so that small, night blue borders
protrude from the pattern paper. Stick the
embroideries behind the openings. Stick the
pattern paper on a square, carnation white
double card (13 x 13 cm). Stick part of a tassel
on the card. Cut off the excess and stick it on
the back of the card at exactly the same height.
Use 3D glue or foam tape to stick a button on
the tassel.

Card 4

Take a piece of pattern paper (21 x 15 cm) and
fold it double. Draw a square (4.5 x 4.5 cm) on
the back 3 cm from the sides and the top and
cut it out. Stick night blue card (14.5 x 10 cm)
against the pattern paper. Cut a square out of
the night blue card so that a small, night blue
border protrudes from the pattern paper. Stick
the embroidery behind the opening. Stick the
pattern paper on a carnation white double card
(10.5 x 15 cm). Stick a piece of patchwork paper
on the card. Use 3D glue or foam tape to stick a
button on the piece of patchwork paper.

Houses

The whole world seems white.

Even the clouds, which still

hold some snow.

What you need:
- 3D cutting sheets: houses in the snow
- Pattern paper no. 5 • Papicolor card: iris blue (31) and violet (20) • Fun eyelet tags: open frames • Fun eyelets: metallic dark blue

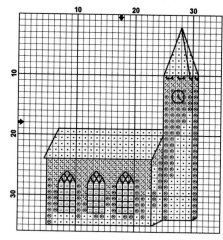

Church and house colour list

•	white (B5200)	=	676
◉	3756	♥	318
%	3747		

Backstitch 1/6 thread
Church and house: 318
Clock, win dows and door: 3799

Card 1

Take a piece of pattern paper (13 x 13 cm). Draw a square (6 x 6 cm) on the back 3.5 cm from all the sides and cut it out. Stick iris blue card (12.5 x 12.5 cm) against the pattern paper. Cut a square out of the iris blue card so that a small, iris blue border protrudes from the pattern paper. Stick the embroidery behind the opening. Stick the pattern paper on a square, violet double card (13 x 13 cm). Use an eyelet to attach an ice crystal eyelet tag.

Card 2

Take a piece of pattern paper (21 x 15 cm) and fold it double. Draw a rectangle (4 x 3 cm) on the back 1.5 cm from the side and 1 cm from the

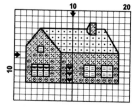

bottom and cut it out. Stick iris blue card (14.5 x 10 cm) against the pattern paper. Cut a rectangle out of the iris blue card so that a small, iris blue border protrudes from the pattern paper. Stick the embroidery behind the opening. Stick the pattern paper on a violet double card (10.5 x

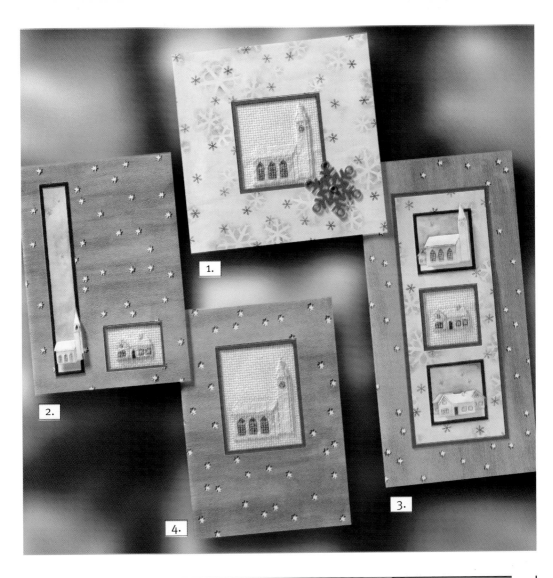

1.

2.

3.

4.

15 cm). Stick a long and narrow picture on the card. Make the church 3D.

Card 3

Cut a square (21 x 21 cm) from violet card and fold it double. Stick a piece of pattern paper (10.5 x 21 cm) on it. Take another piece of pattern paper (6 x 16 cm) and draw a square (4 x 4 cm) on the back 1 cm from the sides and 6 cm from the top and bottom and cut it out. Stick iris blue card (6.5 x 16.5 cm) against the pattern paper. Cut a square out of the iris blue card so that a small, iris blue border protrudes from the pattern paper. Stick the embroidery

behind the opening. Stick the pattern paper on the card. Stick two pictures (middle size) on the card and make the pictures 3D.

Card 4

Take a piece of pattern paper (21 x 15 cm) and fold it double. Draw a rectangle (5.5 x 7 cm) on the back 2.5 cm from the sides and the top and cut it out. Stick iris blue card (14.5 x 10 cm) against the pattern paper. Cut a rectangle out of the iris blue card so that a small, iris blue border protrudes from the pattern paper. Stick the embroidery behind the opening. Stick the pattern paper on a violet double card (10.5 x 15cm).

Christmas decorations

With Christmas just around the corner, embroider Christmas decorations in every colour.

What you need:
• Pattern paper: no. 12 and no. 15 • Scrapbook paper: green patchwork • Papicolor card: carnation white (03), olive green (45) and light green (47) • Gold card • Gold text sticker

Card 1

Take a piece of pattern paper no. 12 (21 x 15 cm) and fold it double. Draw a square (5.5 x 5.5 cm) on the back 2.5 cm from the sides and the top and cut it out. Stick gold card (14.5 x 10 cm) against the pattern paper. Cut a square out of the gold card so that a small, gold border protrudes from the pattern paper. Stick the embroidery behind the opening. Stick the pattern paper on a carnation white double card (10.5 x 15 cm).

Green Christmas decoration colour list

- • 746
- O 415
- = 3072
- % 3053
- ✦ 3051

Backstitch 1/6 thread
Crown: 414
Around the decoration: 3051
For a sparkling result: go over the three grey crosses with silver thread.

Yellow Christmas decoration colour list

- • 746
- = 677
- ◉ 3046
- ● 833

Backstitch 1/6 thread
Crown: 414
Around the Christmas decoration: 833
Along the curls: gold thread

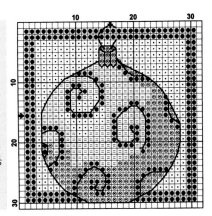

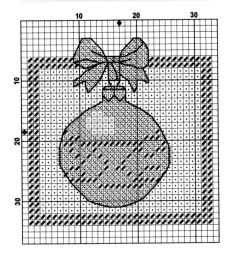

against the pattern paper. Cut a rectangle out of the olive green card so that a small, olive green border protrudes from the pattern paper. Stick the embroidery behind the opening. Stick the pattern paper on a light green double card (10.5 x 15 cm). Stick a piece of patchwork paper on the card. Use 3D glue or foam tape to stick a button on the piece of patchwork paper.

Card 3

Take a piece of pattern paper no. 15 (13 x 13 cm). Draw a square (6 x 6 cm) on the back 3.5 cm from all the sides and cut it out. Stick olive green card (12.5 x 12.5 cm) against the pattern paper. Cut a square out of the olive green card so that a small, olive green border protrudes from the pattern paper. Stick the embroidery behind the opening. Stick the pattern paper on a light green double card (13 x 13 cm). Stick four pieces of patchwork paper on the card.

Card 2

Take a piece of pattern paper no. 15 (21 x 15 cm) and fold it double. Draw a rectangle (4.5 x 6 cm) on the back 3 cm from the sides and the top and cut it out. Stick olive green card (14.5 x 10 cm)

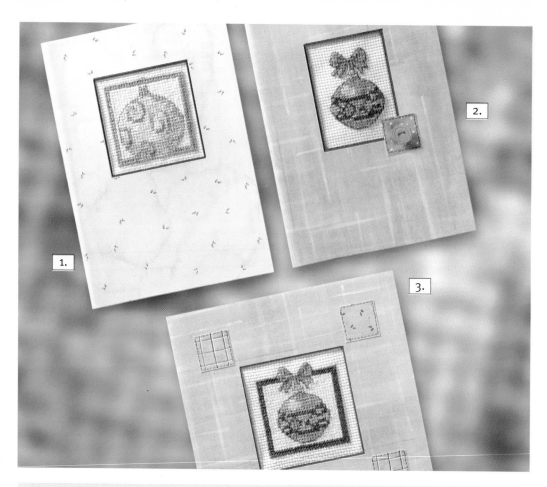

The materials used can be ordered by shopkeepers from:
• Kars & Co B.V. in Ochten, the Netherlands • Jalekro B.V. in Assendelft, the Netherlands • Papicolor International B.V. in Utrecht, the Netherlands • Vadeko Kreatief in Spijkenisse, the Netherlands • Hobby Totaal in Zwolle, the Netherlands • HOCA in Beek en Donk, the Netherlands • Coats in Ninove, Belgium